Taste of Christmas

Walkin' in a Winter
Candy-Land

© 2013 by Barbour Publishing, Inc.

Compiled by Nanette Anderson in association with Snapdragon Group℠, Tulsa, Oklahoma.

ISBN 978-1-62416-136-0

Published by Barbour Publishing, Inc., P.O. Box 719, Uhrichsville, Ohio 44683, www.barbourbooks.com

Our mission is to publish and distribute inspirational products offering exceptional value and biblical encouragement to the masses.

ecpa Member of the
Evangelical Christian
Publishers Association

Printed in the United States of America.

Taste of Christmas

Walkin' in a Winter Candy-Land

Recipes and Holiday Inspiration for Candy Lovers

BARBOUR
PUBLISHING

And she shall bring forth a son,
and thou shalt call his name Jesus:
for he shall save his people
from their sins.

MATTHEW 1:21 KJV

Contents

Candy! Candy! Candy! . . .

What would Christmas be without it? It's the one time of year when we give ourselves permission to delight in confectionary sweetness in all its decadent forms. That's why we compiled this collection of Christmassy candy goodness. We want to help you indulge your sweet tooth. Who knows? Some of these recipes might even become family favorites in the years to come. So get out that candy thermometer, invest in a roll of waxed paper, and see what you can cook up to sweeten the holiday season.

Suddenly a great company of the heavenly host appeared with the angel, praising God and saying, "Glory to God in the highest heaven, and on earth peace to those on whom his favor rests."

LUKE 2:13–14

Hard Candy & Brittle

O little town of Bethlehem, how still we see thee lie!
Above thy deep and dreamless
sleep the silent stars go by.
Yet in thy dark streets shineth the everlasting Light;
The hopes and fears of all the years
are met in thee tonight.

PHILLIPS BROOKS

Old-Fashioned Vinegar Candy

2 cups sugar
½ cup cider vinegar

2 tablespoons butter
Dash salt

Combine ingredients in 2-quart saucepan and cook to brittle stage (270 degrees). Pour mixture onto buttered surface. When cool enough to handle, roll into small balls and depress each ball to form a disk. Let cool in open air. Wrap each in a candy wrapper.

Yield: 2 dozen

Old-Fashioned Hoarhound Candy

3½ pounds brown sugar
½ teaspoon salt

3 cups hot water
1 tablespoon hoarhound extract

Cook sugar, salt, and water to hard-ball stage (265 degrees). Remove from heat and stir in flavoring. Pour onto greased cookie sheet. When completely cool, break into slivers.

Yield: about 150 pieces

Cinnamon Candies

1½ cups sugar
2 cups light corn syrup
Dash salt

Red food coloring
8 to 10 drops cinnamon oil or extract
Powdered sugar

Combine sugar, corn syrup, salt, and food coloring. Bring to boil and cook to hard-crack stage (300 degrees), or when a spoonful forms brittle ribbons in cold water. Remove from heat and add flavoring. Stir well. Pour onto buttered cookie sheet and allow to harden and cool completely. Then press a heavy weight into middle of pan to begin slivering the candy. Toss bite-size slivers in bag of powdered sugar. Shake off excess.

Yield: about 1 pound

Maple Hard Candy

3½ cups sugar
1 cup light corn syrup
1 cup water

½ teaspoon salt
4 tablespoons maple extract
Powdered sugar

Combine first 4 ingredients in heavy saucepan and cook over medium heat until mixture reaches hard-crack stage (300 degrees), or when brittle strands form in cold water. Stir occasionally. Remove from heat and stir in maple flavoring. Pour into buttered jelly roll pan or well greased, individual candy molds. Allow to cool. If you've chosen the jelly roll pan route, press in middle of candy and it should shatter. If molds are used, pop candies out when cool. Tip: A light dusting of powdered sugar will keep candy pieces from sticking together in an airtight storage container.

Yield: 1½ pounds

Peppermint Drops

1½ cups sugar
2 cups light corn syrup
Dash salt

Red food coloring
8 to 10 drops peppermint oil or extract

Combine sugar, corn syrup, salt, and food coloring. Bring to boil and cook to hard-crack stage (300 degrees), or when a spoonful forms brittle ribbons in cold water. Remove from heat and add flavoring. Stir well. Pour onto buttered cookie sheet and allow to harden and cool completely. Then press a heavy weight into middle of pan to begin slivering the candy.

Yield: about 1 pound

Santa's Coffee Drops

1½ cups sugar
2 cups dark corn syrup
Dash salt

4 to 6 teaspoons instant coffee
granules (or to taste)

Combine sugar, corn syrup, salt, and coffee granules. Bring to boil and cook to hard-crack stage (300 degrees), or when a spoonful forms brittle ribbons in cold water. Pour onto buttered cookie sheet and allow to harden and cool completely. Then press a heavy weight into middle of pan to begin slivering the candy.

Yield: about 1 pound

Mexican Orange Drops

3 cups sugar
1½ cups light cream
Grated rinds of 2 large oranges

½ cup butter
½ teaspoon salt
1 cup finely chopped nuts

Caramelize 1 cup of sugar in heavy saucepan (stir sugar in pan over medium heat until it liquefies and turns golden). Add cream to sugar and stir over medium heat until all grains of sugar are melted. Add remaining 2 cups of sugar and cook mixture to hard-ball stage (265 degrees). Remove from heat and add orange rind, butter, salt, and nuts. Pour into 8 x 11-inch buttered pan and cool slightly before cutting into cubes.

Yield: 3 dozen

Lemon Joys

1½ cups sugar
2 cups light corn syrup
Dash salt

Yellow food coloring
8 to 10 drops lemon extract

Combine sugar, corn syrup, salt, and food coloring. Bring to boil and cook to hard-crack stage (300 degrees), or when a spoonful forms brittle ribbons in cold water. Remove from heat and add flavoring. Stir well. Pour into small disk candy molds treated with non-stick cooking spray and allow to set. Turn out and wrap each in a candy wrapper to store.

Yield: about 1 pound

Almond Roca

1 cup butter
1 cup sugar
½ teaspoon salt
2 tablespoons light corn syrup

1 (12 ounce) bag milk chocolate chips
1 (12 ounce) bag butterscotch chips
½ cup almonds, finely chopped

In medium saucepan, combine butter, sugar, salt, and corn syrup. Bring to soft boil for 10 minutes or until syrup reaches 300 degrees. Pour into greased jelly roll pan and sprinkle baking chips evenly. When chips are melted, spread them around with a knife. Immediately sprinkle nuts on top and refrigerate. Break into pieces when hard.

Yield: 2 dozen pieces

English Yuletide Toffee

1½ cups brown sugar
1 cup (2 sticks) butter

1 cup finely chopped nuts
1 cup milk chocolate chips

In heavy saucepan, cook brown sugar and butter to hard-ball stage (265 degrees). Grease small pan and arrange half of the nuts in the bottom. Pour hot syrup over nuts to depth of ½ inch. When partially set, but still very warm, spread chocolate chips over top and allow them to melt. Then use a knife to spread melted chocolate evenly over toffee. Sprinkle with remaining nuts and allow to harden. Then break into pieces and store in airtight container.

Yield: about 24 pieces

Shepherd's Toffee

Saltine crackers
1 cup brown sugar

1 cup butter
1 (12 ounce) bag milk chocolate chips

Line 9 x 13-inch baking pan with foil. Lightly coat with butter, then cover with single layer of crackers. Mix brown sugar and butter in saucepan and bring to light boil for 3 minutes. Drizzle over crackers and bake at 400 degrees for 5 minutes. Remove from oven and immediately sprinkle with chocolate chips. Wait until chips are very soft, then spread evenly with spatula. Refrigerate until set and cut into small pieces.

Yield: 2 dozen pieces

Peanut Brittle

2 cups sugar
1 cup light corn syrup
½ cup water
3 cups raw peanuts

1 teaspoon melted butter
1 teaspoon baking soda
1 teaspoon vanilla
Dash salt

Combine sugar, corn syrup, and water in 2-quart saucepan. Bring to easy boil and cook to soft-ball stage (236 degrees). Add peanuts and butter until mixture reaches 290 degrees and is light brown color. Remove from burner and add in baking soda and vanilla. Stir while mixture cools and thickens. Pour onto buttered cookie sheet and allow to cool completely. Break into bite-size pieces. Store in an airtight tin or jar.

Yield: 3 dozen pieces

Pecan Brittle

2 cups salted pecans, roughly chopped
½ cup light corn syrup
2 cups water
½ teaspoon salt

1 cup sugar
½ teaspoon baking soda
1 teaspoon vanilla

In heavy saucepan, combine nuts, corn syrup, water, salt, and sugar. Cook to soft-crack stage (300 degrees). Remove from heat and briskly stir in baking soda and vanilla. Pour onto buttered cookie sheet, spread evenly, and allow to harden. When cool, break into pieces and store in airtight container.

Yield: 1 pound

Pine Nut Brittle

1 cup sugar
¼ cup water

¼ teaspoon salt
¼ cup pine nuts

Stir sugar and water in heavy saucepan over medium heat until sugar dissolves. Increase heat and boil syrup until it is a deep golden color. Immediately pour mixture into jelly roll pan and sprinkle with pine nuts. Cool completely before breaking into bite-size pieces.

Yield: 2 dozen

Microwave Peanut Brittle

1 cup peanuts
1 cup sugar
½ cup light corn syrup
Dash salt

1 tablespoon butter
1 teaspoon baking soda
1 teaspoon vanilla

In microwaveable bowl, combine first 4 ingredients, mixing well. Microwave on high for 3 minutes. Stir in butter. Microwave for 5 to 6 minutes, stirring occasionally. Remove from microwave. Add baking soda and vanilla. Beat until light and foamy. Pour into greased pan and spread thin. Allow to cool and harden before turning out onto dry surface to break into pieces.

Yield: 1 pound

Rocky Road Fudge Brittle

6 regular-size quality chocolate bars
1 cup coarsely chopped nuts

2 cups miniature marshmallows

Melt chocolate bars until smooth. Stir in nuts and marshmallows. Pour onto greased baking sheet and allow to harden. Then break into pieces.

Yield: ½ pound

Cranberry Bark

1 pint dried cranberries
1 pound good melting white chocolate

1 tablespoon vegetable shortening
Dash salt

Spread dried cranberries evenly on parchment paper–lined cookie sheet. Slowly melt white chocolate, shortening, and salt in heavy saucepan. When smooth, pour mixture evenly over fruit and allow to set. Break into pieces.

Yield: 1 pound

Fudge, Pralines & Clusters

Time was with most of us, when Christmas Day,

encircling all our limited world like a magic ring,

left nothing out for us to miss or seek;

bound together all our home enjoyments, affections,

and hopes; grouped everything and everyone round the

Christmas fire, and made the little picture shining

in our bright young eyes complete.

CHARLES DICKENS

Never-Fail Chocolate Peanut Butter Fudge

2 cups milk chocolate chips
2 tablespoons creamy peanut butter

½ (14 ounce) can sweetened
    condensed milk
Dash salt
1 cup chopped pecans

In heavy saucepan, combine chocolate chips, peanut butter, milk, and salt. Stirring constantly over low heat, melt until smooth. Remove from heat and stir in nuts. Pour into parchment-lined, 9-inch square dish and chill. Invert onto cutting board, remove paper, and cut into cubes.

Yield: 2 dozen

Easy Coconut Fudge

2 cups vanilla-flavored baking chips
1 (14 ounce) can sweetened
    condensed milk

Dash salt
1 cup flaked coconut

In heavy saucepan, stir together vanilla baking chips, milk, and salt over low heat. When smooth, remove from heat and stir in coconut. Pour into parchment-lined, 9-inch square dish and chill. Invert onto cutting board, remove paper, and cut into cubes.

Yield: 2 dozen

Easy Christmas Fudge

1 stick butter, melted
1 can evaporated milk
1½ cups sugar
¼ teaspoon salt

1 (7 ounce) jar marshmallow cream
1 (12 ounce) bag semisweet chocolate
  chips
1 teaspoon vanilla

In heavy saucepan, combine butter, milk, sugar, salt, and marshmallow cream over low heat. Bring mixture to soft boil, stirring constantly, for 5 minutes. Remove from heat and add chips and vanilla. Stir until chocolate is melted. Pour into 7 x 11-inch, parchment-lined baking dish and allow to cool. (Nuts of your choice may be added along with chocolate chips.) Cut into squares and store covered.

Yield: 2 dozen

No-Cook Peanut Butter Fudge

2 ounces baking chocolate
½ cup peanut butter
⅔ cup evaporated milk

2 cups powdered sugar
¼ cup chopped nuts

Melt chocolate in microwave. Add peanut butter and milk and stir until smooth. Add sugar and nuts, and using hands, knead gently until soft roll can be formed. Wrap in waxed paper and chill. Cut in rounds to serve.

Yield: 2 dozen

No-Cook Maple Fudge

2 ounces white baking chocolate
½ cup maple syrup
¼ cup evaporated milk

2 cups powdered sugar
¼ cup chopped nuts
Dash salt

Melt white baking chocolate in microwave. Add maple syrup and milk and stir until smooth. Add sugar and nuts and, using hands, knead gently until soft roll can be formed. Wrap in waxed paper and chill. Cut in rounds to serve.

Yield: 2 dozen

Never Fail Dark Chocolate Fudge

3 cups semisweet or bittersweet
   chocolate chips
1 (14 ounce) can sweetened
   condensed milk

Dash salt
1 cup chopped nuts
1 teaspoon vanilla

Stir chips, milk, and salt over very low heat until smooth and melted. Remove from burner and add nuts and vanilla. Spread mixture into buttered, 8-inch square pan. Chill until firm. Turn out onto flat surface and cut into squares. Store in airtight container.

Yield: 2 dozen

Snowy Day Fudge

¾ cup cocoa
3 cups sugar
1½ cups whole milk
½ teaspoon salt

2 tablespoons butter
2 teaspoons vanilla
2 cups walnut pieces

In heavy saucepan, combine cocoa, sugar, milk, and salt. Bring to soft boil and maintain it until mixture reaches soft-ball stage (236 degrees). Remove from burner and stir in butter, vanilla, and nuts. Let cool for 10 minutes. Beat mixture until it is creamy-thick and adheres to spoon. Transfer to buttered, 8-inch square pan to set up. Cut into squares.

Yield: 2 dozen

Oreo Fudge

18 ounces white baking chocolate
1 (14 ounce) can sweetened
condensed milk

2 dashes salt
2 cups coarsely crushed Oreos

In heavy saucepan, combine white chocolate, milk, and salt, stirring constantly over low heat until smooth and pourable. Remove from burner and quickly stir in crushed cookies. Pour into well-greased, 8- or 9-inch square pan and chill to harden. Turn out onto cutting board and cut into cubes.

Yield: 2 dozen

Snow Fudge

2 cups sugar
1 cup evaporated milk
1 stick butter
1 cup white chocolate chips

½ cup flaked coconut
½ cup chopped pecans
1 teaspoon vanilla
Dash salt

In heavy saucepan, cook sugar, milk, and butter over medium heat to soft-ball stage (236 degrees), stirring constantly. Remove from heat and let stand 10 minutes. Add white chocolate and stir until melted. Quickly add in coconut, pecans, vanilla, and salt. Spread into buttered, 8 x 8-inch pan. Cool and cut into squares.

Yield: 1 pound

Blizzard Fudge

3 cups semisweet chocolate chips
1 (14 ounce) can sweetened
  condensed milk
½ stick butter, divided

¼ teaspoon salt
1 teaspoon vanilla
1 cup chopped nuts
2 cups miniature marshmallows

In heavy saucepan, combine chocolate chips, condensed milk, half the butter, and salt. Heat gently until melted and smooth, stirring constantly. Add vanilla and nuts and pour into greased 8 x 8-inch dish. In fresh saucepan, melt marshmallows and remaining butter. Pour over fudge in dish. Use a knife to swirl white and dark together gently. Chill and cut into squares.

Yield: 2 dozen

Low-Fat Mocha Fudge

3 cups semisweet chocolate chips
1 (14 ounce) can low-fat sweetened
  condensed milk
¼ cup hot fudge ice cream topping

2 teaspoons coffee crystals
½ teaspoon salt
1 teaspoon vanilla

In heavy saucepan, stir together chocolate chips and condensed milk over low heat until melted and smooth. Add ice cream topping, coffee, salt, and vanilla. Pour into parchment paper–lined 8-inch square dish. Refrigerate for an hour. Then turn out onto cutting board, remove paper, and cut into cubes.

Yield: 2½ dozen

Elfishly Good Fudge Roll

2 cups sugar
4 tablespoons cocoa
Dash salt
2 tablespoons flour

1 cup water
1 teaspoon vanilla
3 tablespoons butter
1 cup finely chopped nuts (optional)

Combine sugar, cocoa, salt, flour, and water in heavy saucepan. Cook to soft-ball stage (236 degrees). Remove from heat and add vanilla and butter. Pour into greased pan and allow to cool to lukewarm. Then beat or knead candy until it is soft and creamy. Add nuts if desired. Form into roll and chill wrapped in plastic. Slice to serve.

Yield: 2 dozen slices

Graham Cracker Pralines

24 graham crackers (double rectangles)
¾ stick butter
¾ stick margarine

1 cup light brown sugar
Dash salt
1 cup chopped pecans

Place graham crackers, as close as possible, on greased jellyroll pan. Boil butter, margarine, sugar, and salt for 2 minutes. Remove from heat and add pecans. Immediately spread over graham crackers and bake at 350 degrees for 10 minutes. Watch carefully. When cool, break into pieces and store in airtight container.

Yield: 1 pound

Mimi's Pecan Pralines

3 cups sugar
1 cup milk
2 tablespoons light corn syrup

1 teaspoon vanilla
1 tablespoon butter
3 cups pecan halves

In heavy saucepan, combine sugar, milk, and corn syrup. Cook to soft-ball stage (236 degrees), or when spoonful of mixture forms a soft ball in cold water. Remove from heat and beat in vanilla, butter, and pecans. Stir until mixture begins to thicken and turn opaque. Very quickly drop by spoonfuls onto waxed paper to harden.

Yield: 3 dozen

Deep South Pralines

2 cups packed dark brown sugar
1 cup granulated sugar
¼ teaspoon salt
⅓ cup whole milk

3 cups pecan halves
2 tablespoons butter
1 teaspoon vanilla

In heavy saucepan, combine sugars, salt, and milk and cook to soft-ball stage (236 degrees). Add pecans, butter, and vanilla. Return just to rolling boil and then remove from heat. Beat until mixture begins to thicken and cloud. (This will happen very quickly!) Drop by spoonfuls onto waxed paper. When completely cool and hard, store in airtight container.

Yield: 2 dozen

Easy Pecan Turtles

3 cups small pecan halves
1 (11 ounce) bag pre-wrapped
   caramels

1 (12 ounce) bag milk chocolate chips
Dash salt
1 tablespoon vegetable shortening

On large, parchment-lined cookie sheet, arrange pecans in individual 3-nut pods like a pinwheel. Unwrap and melt caramels according to instructions on bag. Spoon warm and slightly rethickening caramel over each pecan pod in a plump mound. Allow to cool and set. Melt chocolate chips, salt, and shortening together. When smooth, pour over each candy just to cover. Leave to cool and harden.

Yield: 2 dozen

Wonderland Hazelnut Clusters

3½ cups corn or rice squares cereal
¾ cup coarsely-chopped toasted
   hazelnuts
1 cup milk chocolate chips

½ cup chocolate-hazelnut spread
½ teaspoon salt
1 cup powdered sugar

In large bowl, combine cereal and chopped nuts. Set aside. Melt together chocolate chips, chocolate-hazelnut spread, and salt. When smooth, pour over cereal mixture and stir until coated. Turn mixture out onto buttered surface and allow to cool. Break apart into clusters, then sprinkle with powdered sugar.

Yield: 1 pound

Macadamia Clusters

1 cup sugar
1 cup dark corn syrup
3 tablespoons butter

1 cup light cream
1 teaspoon vanilla
1½ cups salted macadamia nuts

In heavy saucepan, combine all ingredients except nuts and cook to hard-ball stage (265 degrees), stirring occasionally. Remove from burner and stir in vanilla and nuts. Spoon into individual candy wrappers and allow to harden.

Yield: 1 pound

Almond Coconut Clusters

2 cups sugar
½ cup milk
1 tablespoon light corn syrup
1 cup unsweetened flaked coconut

1 cup toasted almond slivers
1 teaspoon vanilla
1 teaspoon butter
Dash salt

In heavy saucepan, combine sugar, milk, and corn syrup. Cook to soft-ball stage (236 degrees) and remove from heat. Add coconut, almonds, vanilla, butter, and salt. Stir vigorously until mixture begins to cream and thicken. Working quickly, drop by spoonfuls onto waxed paper.

Yield: 2 dozen

White Chocolate Nut Clusters

1 (12 ounce) bag white chocolate chips
1 tablespoon shortening

2 cups salted mixed nuts
½ cup flaked coconut

In heavy saucepan, slowly melt chocolate and shortening, stirring constantly. When creamy smooth, add in nuts and coconut. Drop by spoonfuls onto waxed paper to set.

Yield: 2 dozen

Trail Mix Clusters

½ (6 ounce) bag chocolate chips
¼ cup chunky peanut butter
1 (14 ounce) can sweetened
   condensed milk
Dash salt

1 teaspoon vanilla
2 cups granola
1 cup chopped nuts
½ cup dried cranberries or raisins

In heavy saucepan, combine chocolate chips, peanut butter, milk, and salt. Stir over medium heat until smooth. Mix in vanilla, granola, nuts, and fruit. Drop by spoonfuls onto waxed paper to set.

Yield: 2 dozen

Peanut Praline Patties

3 cups sugar
1 cup whole milk
2 tablespoons light corn syrup
½ teaspoon salt

1 teaspoon vanilla
Red food coloring (enough to shade
mixture bright pink)
2 cups unsalted Spanish peanuts

Cook sugar, milk, corn syrup, and salt to soft-ball stage (236 degrees). Remove from heat and stir in vanilla, food coloring, and peanuts. Beat mixture just until you sense thickening and very slight opaqueness. Drop quickly into round patties onto sheet of parchment or waxed paper.

Yield: 2 dozen

Maple Sugar Candy

2 cups maple syrup   Dash salt

Bring both ingredients to very low boil. Cook to soft-ball stage (236 degrees).
Remove from heat, leaving candy thermometer in mixture until it cools to 100
degrees. Beat mixture until it starts to look creamy. Pour into maple leaf or
other candy molds and allow to set.

Yield: 2 dozen

Candy Creams, Bites & Chews

For he himself is our peace.

EPHESIANS 2:14

Christmas Butter Creams

2 cups powdered sugar
½ stick soft butter
1 tablespoon whole milk

1 teaspoon vanilla
Dash salt
8 ounces dipping chocolate

Cream together sugar and butter. Add in milk, vanilla, and salt. Roll into small, mint-size shapes and dip into melted chocolate. Coat well and set on waxed paper to harden.

Yield: 2 dozen

Chocolate-Covered Pineapple Creams

1 cup heavy cream
1 cup sugar
½ cup light corn syrup
⅔ cup well-drained pineapple
Dash salt
1 tablespoon butter

1 teaspoon vanilla
2 cups chocolate chips (white,
    semisweet, or milk chocolate may
    be used)
1 tablespoon vegetable shortening

In heavy saucepan, bring first 5 ingredients to gentle boil and cook to soft-ball stage (236 degrees). Stir in butter and vanilla. When lukewarm, turn mixture out onto buttered surface and form into 1-inch balls. Melt chocolate and shortening together and dip each ball until coated. (Use toothpicks to swirl balls in chocolate, then remove them as you set each ball on waxed paper to harden.)

Yield: 2 dozen

Peppermint Creams

2 cups sugar
¼ cup light corn syrup
¼ cup milk
¼ teaspoon cream of tartar

¼ teaspoon salt
10 drops peppermint extract
Red food coloring

Bring first 5 ingredients to boil in heavy saucepan. Cook to soft-ball stage (236 degrees). Remove from heat, stir in flavoring, and beat until creamy, adding red food coloring until pink. Drop by spoonfuls into Christmas candy forms or by dollops onto waxed paper. Let set, then take out of forms and store in covered tin.

Yield: 3 dozen

Dipped Marshmallows

1 (10 ounce) bag marshmallows
6 finely crushed candy canes
1 (12 ounce) bag semisweet or milk
  chocolate chips

1 tablespoon vegetable shortening
Dash salt

Skewer marshmallows on party toothpicks and arrange (not touching) on cookie sheet. Refrigerate for 2 hours. Crush candy canes and spread out on waxed paper. In heavy saucepan, melt chocolate, shortening, and salt. Dip each cool marshmallow in melted chocolate mixture, shaking off excess before rolling in peppermint to coat. Return to refrigerator to set.

Yield: About 30 treats

Holiday Maple Creams

½ cup butter
1¾ cups brown sugar
2 eggs
1 teaspoon maple flavoring
1½ cups flour

2 teaspoon baking powder
½ cup nuts (optional)
½ pound white dipping chocolate
  (melted)

Cream together butter and sugar. Add eggs and flavoring. Combine flour and baking powder and blend into creamed mixture. Fold in nuts. Form into balls and bake at 350 degrees on greased cookie sheet for 25 to 30 minutes. Cool well. Dip each ball into white chocolate, and allow to set on waxed paper.

Yield: 2 dozen

Swedish Crème Candy

2 (6 ounce) packages of unflavored
    gelatin
2 tablespoons cold water
1 cup sugar
1 cup heavy whipping cream

Dash salt
½ cup sour cream
1 teaspoon vanilla
Dried fruit or nuts

In heavy saucepan, let gelatin soak in cold water for 5 minutes. Add sugar, whipping cream, and salt. Cook over medium heat, stirring constantly, until gelatin is dissolved. Remove from heat and add sour cream and vanilla. Whisk until smooth and pour into lightly greased, 9-inch square dish. Sprinkle with dried fruit or nuts and refrigerate until well-set. Keep refrigerated and cut into cubes as ready to serve.

Yield: 3 dozen

No-Bake Chocolate Drops

2 cups sugar
4 tablespoons cocoa
1 stick butter

½ cup milk
1 teaspoon vanilla
3 cups quick-cooking oats

In heavy saucepan, combine first 5 ingredients and cook, stirring for 2 minutes. Remove from heat and add oats. Mix well and drop by spoonfuls onto waxed paper to harden. Add 1 cup peanut butter or ½ cup coconut along with oats for variety.

Yield: 2 dozen

Christmas Clouds

½ cup water

2 cups brown sugar

2 egg whites (beaten until stiff)

½ cup walnut halves

In 2-quart saucepan, cook water and sugar to hard-ball stage (265 degrees). Remove from heat and add gradually to egg whites, beating until mixture is creamy. Drop by spoonfuls onto waxed paper and press walnut half into each piece.

Yield: 2 dozen

Spearmint Clouds

2 cups sugar
½ cup light corn syrup
½ cup water

Dash salt
1 egg white (beaten)
½ teaspoon spearmint extract

Combine all ingredients except egg white and extract in 2-quart saucepan and cook to hard-ball stage (265 degrees). Remove from burner and add gradually to egg white. Stir in flavoring. Beat until creamy and drop in mounds on waxed paper.

Yield: 2 dozen

Winter Delights

3 tablespoons unflavored gelatin
2 cups sugar
1 cup water, divided
Grated rind and strained juice of one
 orange

Grated rind and strained juice of one
 lemon
Dash salt
Red or green food coloring

Stir gelatin into ½ cup cold water and allow to soften while you heat sugar and ½ cup water in small, heavy saucepan. Cook slowly for about 8 minutes, then add gelatin mixture. Cook for another 10 minutes and remove from heat. Stir in rind, juice, salt, and coloring of your choice. Pour into greased pan to the depth of one inch. Cool and cut into cubes. (You may add 1 cup of chopped nuts to the mixture before pouring, if desired.)

Yield: 2 to 3 dozen

Peanut Butter Kisses

1 cup dark corn syrup
1 cup crunchy peanut butter
1½ cups dried milk flakes

1 cup powdered sugar
3 cups crispy rice cereal

Combine corn syrup and peanut butter. Alternately add in dry milk and sugar until dough is smooth. Add cereal one cup at a time, mixing well with each addition. With buttered hands, form dough into balls and set on waxed paper to harden.

Yield: 2 dozen

Chocolate Coconut Chews

3 cups chocolate chips, divided
1½ cups shredded coconut
1 (14 ounce) can sweetened
   condensed milk

1 cup macadamia nuts (unsalted)
1 cup fresh white bread crumbs
Dash salt
2 tablespoons vegetable shortening

In large bowl, mix together 1 cup chocolate chips with coconut, condensed milk, nuts, bread crumbs, and salt. Let mixture sit at room temperature for 1 hour. Form into 2-inch balls and place back in bowl. Cover and leave at room temperature overnight. In the morning, melt remaining 2 cups chocolate chips along with shortening in a heavy saucepan. When smooth, dip each ball and shake off excess. Set on waxed paper to harden. This may take several hours.

Yield: 2 dozen

Peanut Butter Holiday Chewies

¾ cup light cream
2 cups brown sugar
3 tablespoons peanut butter

Dash salt
1 teaspoon vanilla

Combine ingredients in heavy saucepan and cook to soft-ball stage (235 degrees) or until spoonful of mixture forms soft ball in cold water. Remove from heat and allow to cool to lukewarm. Beat until mixture can be shaped into little logs. When hardened, wrap in candy wrappers and twist the ends.

Yield: 2 to 3 dozen

Mango Chews

1 cup finely chopped dried mango
1 cup finely chopped pecans
½ teaspoon salt

½ (14 ounce) can sweetened
    condensed milk
¾ cup flaked coconut

Combine all ingredients except coconut until mixture can be rolled into 1- to 2-inch balls. Roll balls in coconut and store in refrigerator.

Yield: 2 dozen

Santa's Favorite Molasses Chews

2 cups brown sugar
1 cup molasses
1 tablespoon butter
1 tablespoon white vinegar

½ teaspoon salt
⅛ teaspoon baking soda
1 cup chopped nuts

Combine all ingredients except baking soda and nuts in heavy saucepan. Cook to hard-ball stage (265 degrees) or until spoonful of mixture forms a hard ball in cold water. Remove from heat and stir in baking soda. Add nuts and pour mixture into buttered jelly roll pan. Cut into squares while still warm, then cool.

Yield: 3 dozen

No-Pull Taffy

4 cups sugar
¾ cup light corn syrup
¼ cup water
1½ tablespoons butter

1 teaspoon marshmallow cream
2 drops red food coloring
½ teaspoon peppermint oil
Powdered sugar

Combine sugar, corn syrup, water, and butter in large, heavy saucepan over medium heat. Bring to boil and cook to hard-ball stage (265 degrees). Remove from burner and add marshmallow cream, food coloring, and peppermint oil and stir vigorously as mixture thickens. Pour onto greased surface and press very small cookie cutter Christmas shapes into the candy. Leave them until candy hardens. Gently remove cutters or pop candy out. Dust lightly with powdered sugar.

Yield: 3 dozen

Mexican Taffy

1 cup honey
1 cup finely ground almonds
2 egg yolks
1 teaspoon cinnamon

Dash salt
¼ teaspoon lemon zest
1 egg white (beaten stiff)

In heavy saucepan, slowly heat honey to 140 degrees on candy thermometer. Remove from heat and stir in ground almonds, egg yolks, cinnamon, salt, and lemon zest. When well blended, carefully fold in egg white. Pour onto parchment-lined cookie sheet and smooth out to ½-inch thickness. Place another sheet of parchment paper on top and then put large cutting board on top of second layer of parchment paper. Add a heavy weight to cause an even press on the candy. Set aside for 2 to 3 days. Peel parchment away and cut into bite-size pieces.

Yield: 1 pound

Saltwater Taffy

1 cup light corn syrup
2 cups sugar
¾ cup water

1 tablespoon corn starch
1 tablespoon butter
1 teaspoon salt

Combine ingredients in heavy saucepan and cook to hard-ball stage (265 degrees). Pour mixture onto greased surface and let cool until it can be handled. With lightly buttered hands, begin to pull and stretch taffy until stiff. Stretch into a rope and use kitchen shears to cut into small pieces.

Yield: About 25 pieces

Butterscotch Caramels

3 cups brown sugar
1 stick butter
½ cup water

Dash salt
1 teaspoon vanilla

Combine all ingredients except vanilla in 2-quart saucepan. Stir over low heat until components are dissolved. Increase heat to medium and cook to hard-ball stage (245 degrees), or until spoonful of mixture forms a firm ball when dropped into cold water. Add vanilla. Pour into buttered 9 x 13-inch pan and cool. Cut into cubes and wrap each in candy wrapper.

Yield: 3 dozen

Chocolate Caramels

1 cup sugar
1 cup light corn syrup
½ teaspoon salt

1 cup heavy cream, divided
1 (12 ounce) bag milk chocolate chips

In heavy saucepan, bring sugar, corn syrup, and salt to soft-ball stage (236 degrees). Stir in half the cream and all the chocolate. Bring back to soft-ball stage. Add remaining cream and bring mixture to firm-ball stage (245 degrees). Pour mixture into 8- or 9-inch square, buttered pan and allow to cool and set. Later, turn the block onto greased surface and cut into cubes.

Yield: 2 dozen

Honey Caramels

1 cup honey
¾ cup heavy cream
Dash salt

1 teaspoon vanilla
2 tablespoons butter

In heavy saucepan, bring honey, cream, and salt to soft-ball stage (236 degrees), stirring constantly. Remove from heat and stir in vanilla and butter. Pour into well-buttered, 8 x 8-inch dish. Refrigerate until chilled, several hours.

Yield: 2 dozen

Non-Dairy Caramels

3 cups sugar
1½ cups light corn syrup
2 cups non-dairy creamer

½ teaspoon salt
½ teaspoon vanilla

Combine all ingredients except vanilla and cook in heavy saucepan to soft-ball stage (236 degrees), stirring constantly. Remove from heat and add vanilla. Pour into plastic wrap–lined, 8 x 8-inch baking dish. Refrigerate overnight and cut into cubes.

Yield: 2½ dozen

Little Cornflake Gems

1 cup sugar
1 cup light corn syrup
1 cup peanut butter

5 cups cornflakes cereal
1 teaspoon salt

In large, heavy saucepan, bring sugar and corn syrup to a boil, stirring constantly. Remove from heat and stir in peanut butter. Blend well before adding cereal and salt. Mix and drop by spoonfuls onto waxed paper to set up.

Yield: 2 dozen

Ritzy Bits

2 rolls Ritz-style crackers
½ cup crunchy peanut butter
2 (12 ounce) bags chocolate chips

2 tablespoons vegetable shortening

Sandwich crunchy peanut butter between two crackers. Melt chocolate chips together with vegetable shortening to make dipping mixture. Coat cracker cookies with chocolate, shaking off excess before letting them harden on waxed paper.

Yield: About 2 dozen

Christmas Cake Bites

1 (15.25 ounce) yellow cake mix
1 (16 ounce) can frosting

1 pound melting chocolate for dipping
Christmas cookie decorations

Prepare cake as directed. When completely cool, crumble cake into large bowl and add frosting. Blend well with low-speed mixer until a fine, moist, crumbly mixture is produced. Freeze for 30 minutes. Form into two-inch balls and freeze another 30 minutes. Dip into melted chocolate, and sprinkle with a few cookie decorations. Set on waxed paper to harden.

Yield: 3 dozen

Butterscotch Brownie Bites

¼ cup shortening
1 cup brown sugar
1 egg
½ teaspoon vanilla
1 cup flour

½ teaspoon baking powder
½ teaspoon salt
1 (12 ounce) bag milk chocolate chips
1 tablespoon vegetable shortening

Cream together shortening and sugar. Add egg and vanilla. Mix well. Combine flour, baking powder, and salt and add to creamed mixture. Spread into greased and floured 8-inch square pan and bake at 350 degrees for 20 to 25 minutes. Cool and cut into bite-size cubes. Melt chocolate chips and shortening together and dip each cube into chocolate to coat. Set on waxed paper to harden.

Yield: 3 dozen

Kris Kringle Bites

1 cup sugar
1 cup light corn syrup
½ teaspoon salt
1 cup peanut butter

5 to 6 cups cornflakes cereal
1 (12 ounce) package milk chocolate
   chips
3 ounces butterscotch chips

Boil sugar, corn syrup, and salt for 1 to 2 minutes. Remove from heat and stir in peanut butter. When smooth, stir in cereal and press into ungreased 9 x 13-inch pan. Distribute chocolate and butterscotch chips over all and put under broiler until they begin to melt. (Watch carefully!) Remove from oven and spread softened chips evenly over bars. Cool and cut into bite-size pieces. Store in airtight container.

Yield: 3 dozen

7-Layer Chocolate Coconut Bites

1 stick butter
1½ cups finely crushed graham crackers
Dash salt
1 (14 ounce) can sweetened
  condensed milk

2 cups chocolate chips
2 cups butterscotch chips
1 cup chopped nuts
2 cups flaked coconut

Melt butter and stir into graham cracker crumbs and salt. Press into parchment-lined, 9 x 13-inch pan. Pour milk evenly over crust. Combine all the chips and sprinkle half of them evenly over mixture in pan. Now add nut layer, then coconut layer. Finally, sprinkle on remaining chips and press down firmly all over with a spatula. Bake at 350 degrees for 25 minutes or until lightly browned on top. Cool well, lift by parchment handles out of pan and onto cutting board. Cut into cubes.

Yield: 3 dozen

Sesame Seed Nibbles

2 cups sesame seeds
½ cup sunflower seeds
½ cup chopped nuts
1 cup shredded coconut

1 cup honey
1 cup water
1 cup sugar
2 tablespoons butter

Combine seeds, nuts, and coconut in large mixing bowl. Combine next 4 ingredients in heavy saucepan and bring to gentle boil. Cook to hard-ball stage (265 degrees). Pour hot mixture over seed mixture in mixing bowl. Stir well. Pour out onto buttered surface. When just cool enough to form, roll out to ½-inch thickness. Cut into bite-size pieces and wrap in candy wrappers. Store in airtight container.

Yield: About 1½ pounds candy

Balls, Squares & Crisps

Let us now go even unto Bethlehem,
and see this thing which is come to pass,
which the Lord hath made known unto us.

LUKE 2:15 KJV

Gingerbread Balls

1 cup brown sugar
½ cup shortening
1 cup molasses
2 teaspoons baking soda
1 cup hot water
3 cups flour

1 teaspoon ginger
1 teaspoon cinnamon
1 teaspoon allspice
1 teaspoon nutmeg
1 teaspoon salt
2 eggs (beaten)

Icing:
2 cups powdered sugar
1 stick butter, melted

Few drops milk (enough to create
    dipping consistency)
Dash salt

Cream together sugar, shortening, and molasses. Add baking soda and water. In separate bowl, combine flour and all spices and mix well. Stir into wet mixture and add eggs. Bake at 350 degrees in 8 x 11-inch, greased pan for about 25 minutes. Remove from oven and allow to cool until warm enough to handle. Scoop out enough of warm cake to form 2-inch ball. Use your hands to squeeze and pack into firm (not hard) balls. As balls continue to cool, make icing and dip each ball. Allow to set on waxed paper.

Yield: 2 dozen

Lemon Poppy Seed Balls

1 (15.25 ounce) lemon cake mix
1 (3.4 ounce) package instant vanilla
  pudding
1 cup water
4 beaten eggs

½ teaspoon salt
¼ cup poppy seeds
½ cup oil
1 cup powdered sugar

Combine all ingredients in mixer and pour into 9 x 13-inch greased pan. Bake at 325 degrees for 25 to 30 minutes or until toothpick inserted into middle of cake comes out clean. Remove from oven and allow to cool. Scoop out cake and using your hands, squeeze into firm (not hard) two-inch balls. Roll in powdered sugar.

Yield: 3 dozen

Chocolate-Covered Coconut Balls

2 cups powdered sugar
2 cups flaked coconut
½ (14 ounce) can sweetened
   condensed milk

1 teaspoon salt
1 (12 ounce) bittersweet chocolate
   chips
2 tablespoons vegetable shortening

Combine first 4 ingredients in large bowl. Put in refrigerator to cool. Roll into 2-inch balls and return to refrigerator to cool and set for 1 hour. Over low heat, or in microwave, melt together chocolate chips and shortening. Dip each ball in chocolate, shaking off excess. Set on waxed paper to set.

Yield: 2 dozen

Joyful Almond Balls

15 graham crackers, broken up into small chunks

1 (14 ounce) can sweetened condensed milk

1 (6 ounce) bag semisweet chocolate chips

1 cup flaked coconut

½ cup chopped almonds, toasted

Dash salt

Mix all ingredients together. Form into 2-inch balls and bake on parchment-lined cookie sheet at 350 degrees for about 15 minutes.

Yield: 3 dozen

Apricot Yule Balls

8 ounces dried apricots, diced fine
2½ cups flaked coconut

¾ (14 ounce) can sweetened
    condensed milk
1 cup finely chopped pecans

Mix together apricots, coconut, and milk. Shape into 1-inch balls and roll in nuts. Refrigerate.

Yield: 2 dozen

Mrs. Claus's Date Balls

1 pound dates, pitted and chopped
2 cups sugar
2 beaten eggs
½ cup butter
2 dashes salt

1 teaspoon vanilla
3 cups crispy rice cereal
1 cup chopped nuts
1 cup flaked coconut

Combine dates, sugar, eggs, butter, and salt. Cook over low heat until smooth, stirring constantly. Keep mixture below boiling point. Remove from heat and add vanilla. Mix cereal and nuts in large bowl and pour hot mixture into it, stirring to coat. With buttered hands, form into 1-inch balls and roll each in coconut.

Yield: 4 dozen

Mrs. Claus's Famous Rum Balls

2 cups finely crushed graham crackers
2 tablespoons cocoa
1 cup powdered sugar
2 dashes salt

1 cup walnuts, chopped fine
2 tablespoons honey or agave nectar
¼ cup rum flavoring

Combine all ingredients to a good consistency for forming into small balls. Roll 1- to 2-inch balls in dusting of powdered sugar and shake off excess.

Yield: 2 dozen

Snowballs

2 eggs, beaten
1½ sticks butter
1 cup sugar
2 cups graham cracker crumbs

2 cups chopped nuts
1 cup flaked coconut
2½ cups colored miniature
   marshmallows

Cook first three ingredients over medium heat until thickened. Cool and set aside. In large bowl, combine graham cracker crumbs, nuts, coconut, and marshmallows. Pour cooked, cooled mixture over crumb mixture. Mix well. Press into buttered pan and refrigerate for 2 hours. Cut and roll in powdered sugar. Store in refrigerator.

Yield: 2 to 3 dozen

Snowball Surprise

1 (10 ounce) bag miniature
 marshmallows
4 tablespoons butter
Dash salt

5 cups crispy rice cereal
1 (9 ounce) bag variety bite-size candy
 bars
1 cup light flaked coconut (optional)

In heavy saucepan, melt together marshmallows, butter, and salt. Remove from heat and stir in crispy cereal until well-incorporated. Remove from heat and cool enough to handle. Form into tight balls around candy bar. Sprinkle with coconut if desired, and allow to set.

Yield: 3½ dozen

Strawberry Dreams

1 (15.25 ounce) strawberry cake mix
1 (16 ounce) can cream cheese frosting

1 pound white melting chocolate for dipping
Christmas cookie decorations

Prepare cake mix as directed. When completely cool, crumble cake into large bowl and add frosting. Blend well with low-speed mixer until a fine, moist, crumbly mixture is produced. Freeze for 30 minutes. Form into 2-inch balls and freeze another 30 minutes. Dip into melted chocolate and sprinkle with a few cookie decorations. Set on waxed paper to harden.

Yield: 3 dozen

Pecan Buttermilk Squares

2 cups sugar
½ teaspoon salt
1 teaspoon baking soda
1 cup buttermilk

1 tablespoon butter
1 teaspoon vanilla
1 cup chopped pecans

In heavy saucepan, combine sugar, salt, baking soda, and buttermilk. Stirring constantly, cook to soft-ball stage (236 degrees). Remove from heat and allow to cool for about 10 minutes. Then stir in butter, vanilla, and pecans. Pour into well-greased, 8-inch square pan and allow to cool completely before cutting into bite-size squares.

Yield: 2 dozen

Triple-Decker Chocolate Squares

1 stick butter
¼ cup cocoa
½ cup powdered sugar
½ teaspoon salt
1 egg, beaten
1½ teaspoons vanilla
3 cups graham cracker crumbs
½ cup chopped pecans

1 teaspoon cornstarch
1 tablespoon sugar
½ stick butter
¼ cup evaporated milk
1 teaspoon vanilla
2 cups powdered sugar
1 (8 ounce) milk chocolate bar, shaved

Melt butter and add next 7 ingredients. Cook until hot and well blended. Press into lightly buttered 9 x 13-inch pan and set aside. Combine cornstarch and 1 tablespoon sugar. Add to additional melted butter in heavy saucepan. Mix well. Add milk and cook until thick and creamy. When cool, add vanilla and powdered sugar. Blend well and spread over first layer. Melt chocolate bar and drizzle over cream filling. Cut into squares before chocolate is hardened.

Yield: 3 dozen

Chocolate-Dipped Crispy Rice Treats

1 (10 ounce) bag miniature
  marshmallows
4 tablespoons butter

Dash salt
5 cups crispy rice cereal
1 pound chocolate candy, melted

In heavy saucepan, melt together marshmallows, butter, and salt. Remove from heat and stir in crispy cereal until well-incorporated. Press mixture into 9 x 13-inch pan and allow to cool. When hardened, cut into cubes and dip each in melted chocolate. Shake off excess and drain on mesh to set chocolate.

Yield: 3½ dozen

Chocolate Butterscotch Meltaways

½ cup butter, melted
1 cup graham cracker crumbs
1 cup flaked coconut
1 (12 ounce) bag milk chocolate chips

1 (12 ounce) bag butterscotch chips
2 cups chopped pecans
1 (14 oz) can sweetened condensed
   milk

Pour melted butter into 9 x 13-inch baking dish. Evenly sprinkle graham cracker crumbs over butter. Layer remaining ingredients with nuts on top. Drizzle condensed milk over all and bake at 350 degrees for about 25 minutes. Cool and cut into cubes. Store in tightly covered container.

Yield: 3 dozen

Kris Kringle S'mores

1 tube sugar cookie dough
1 cup graham cracker crumbs
1 cup melted butter

1 (12 ounce) bag milk chocolate chips
1 (10 ounce) bag miniature
    marshmallows

Let cookie dough come to room temperature. Mix cracker crumbs and butter into dough. Press into ungreased, 9 x 13-inch baking pan. Bake at 350 degrees until underdone (about 15 minutes). Remove from oven and sprinkle chocolate chips over top. Let stand until melted, then spread evenly over crust. Set oven to broil. Sprinkle marshmallows over chocolate and put under broiler until marshmallows are slightly brown. (Only takes a minute or so.) Cool slightly and cut into bite-size cubes. Serve immediately.

Yield: about 30 pieces

Christmas Buckeyes

2 cups creamy or crunchy peanut butter
½ cup butter
1 pound powdered sugar

3 cups crispy rice cereal
2 (12 ounce) bags milk chocolate chips
2 tablespoons vegetable shortening

In heavy saucepan, melt peanut butter and butter together over low heat, stirring constantly. In large bowl, combine powdered sugar and cereal. Pour melted peanut butter mixture over cereal and blend well, using hands to form ½-inch balls. Melt chocolate chips and shortening together until smooth. Dip balls in chocolate, allowing inner mixture to peek out the top. Set on waxed paper to harden.

Yield: 3½ dozen

Holiday Crispies

1 cup sugar
1 cup light corn syrup
1 cup light cream
4 ounces cornflakes cereal

3 ounces crispy rice cereal
1 cup shredded coconut
1 cup salted peanuts

Bring sugar, corn syrup, and cream to soft-ball stage (236 degrees) in 2-quart saucepan. In large bowl, crush cornflakes and mix with crispy rice cereal, coconut, and peanuts. Pour hot mixture over cereal mixture and blend well. Press into buttered jelly roll pan and cut into squares when cool.

Yield: 4 dozen

Peanut Crispy Candy

¼ cup butter
5 cups miniature marshmallows
½ cup peanut butter

5 cups crispy rice cereal
1 cup dry-roasted peanuts

Melt butter in microwave. Add marshmallows and microwave for 2 minutes, or until very soft, stirring occasionally to encourage melting. Remove from microwave and stir in peanut butter, cereal, and peanuts. Press warm mixture into lightly buttered, 8 x 11-inch dish. Cool and cut into cubes.

Yield: 2 dozen

Candy Bar Yummies

2 cups semisweet chocolate chips
1 tablespoon vegetable shortening
Dash salt

2 full-size candy bars of your choice, chopped
1 (16 ounce) container milk chocolate frosting
1 cup flaked coconut

In heavy saucepan, melt together chocolate chips, shortening, and salt. Remove from heat and gently stir in chopped candy bars and frosting. Working quickly with buttered hands, form into 2-inch balls and roll in coconut to coat. Set on waxed paper to set.

Yield: 2 dozen

Angel Wings

1 cup semisweet chocolate chips
1 teaspoon vegetable shortening
1 egg (beaten)
1 cup powdered sugar

1 cup chopped pecans
1 cup miniature marshmallows
½ teaspoon salt
½ cup flaked coconut

In heavy saucepan, slowly melt chocolate chips and shortening together. While still very hot, whisk in beaten egg. Remove from burner and add powdered sugar, nuts, marshmallows, and salt. Form into 2-inch balls and roll in coconut. Keep refrigerated in airtight container.

Yield: 2 dozen

Christmas Kisses

1½ cups flour
1 teaspoon baking soda
½ teaspoon salt
½ cup shortening
1 egg (beaten)

2 tablespoons whole milk
½ cup brown sugar
1 teaspoon vanilla
½ cup granulated sugar
1 (11 ounce) bag chocolate kisses

Combine all ingredients except granulated sugar and kisses. Form dough into small balls and roll each in granulated sugar. Bake at 350 degrees for 8 to 10 minutes on greased cookie sheet. Remove from oven and immediately press a chocolate kiss into the middle of each cookie. Allow to cool as candy melts.

Yield: 2 dozen

Winter Haystacks

1½ cup semisweet chocolate chips
½ cup peanut butter

2½ cups chow mien noodles
(uncooked)
½ cup peanuts

Melt chocolate and peanut butter together in heavy saucepan. Stir in noodles and peanuts. Drop by tablespoons onto waxed paper and let harden.

Yield: 2 dozen

Rudolph's Favorite Sandwich Cookies

2 (12 ounce) bags chocolate chips
   (white or dark)
2 tablespoons shortening
Dash salt

1 (16 ounce) package of your favorite
   sandwich cookie

In heavy saucepan, melt chocolate chips, shortening, and salt until smooth.
Using a slotted spoon, dip each cookie into chocolate, gently shaking off excess
before setting it to harden on waxed paper. Repeat dipping if you prefer a
heavier coating.

Yield: About 3 dozen

Holiday Chocolate Truffles

2½ cups milk chocolate chips
1 (14 ounce) can sweetened
  condensed milk
½ teaspoon salt

2 teaspoons vanilla
1 cup very finely chopped pecans
½ cup cocoa powder
1 cup powdered sugar

In heavy saucepan, combine chocolate chips, milk, salt, and vanilla. Stirring constantly over low heat, melt to smooth consistency. Add in nuts and chill mixture for several hours. When firm, shape into 2-inch balls. Combine cocoa powder and powdered sugar. Roll each ball in mixture until coated. Return to refrigerator until chilled and firm.

Yield: 2 dozen

Mocha Truffles

½ cup toasted almond slivers

2 (12 ounce) bags semisweet chocolate chips

1 (8 ounce) package softened cream cheese

2½ tablespoons instant coffee crystals

1 tablespoon water

1 pound almond bark

Toast almonds under broiler, tossing once as they brown. (Watch carefully.) Set aside to cool. In heavy saucepan on low heat (or in microwave), melt chocolate chips. In separate bowl, combine cream cheese, coffee crystals, and water. Add to chocolate and beat until smooth. Chill until firm enough to handle. Form into 1- or 2-inch balls and refrigerate for 2 hours. Then carefully melt almond bark and dip each ball, letting excess drip off before setting on waxed paper to harden.

Yield: 4 dozen

Mint Truffles

1 cup semisweet chocolate chips
8 chocolate-covered mint patties
1 teaspoon vegetable shortening
1 cup whipped topping

2½ tablespoons cocoa powder
2½ tablespoons powdered sugar

Melt together chocolate chips, mint patties, and shortening in microwave, stirring occasionally until smooth. Let cool for 15 minutes. Fold in whipped topping and refrigerate until easy to handle. Roll into 1-inch balls and then roll in combined cocoa and powdered sugar. Shake off excess and store in airtight container.

Yield: 2 dozen

Christmas Bark

1 pound almond bark or white
   chocolate
¾ cup dried cranberries or cranberry
   raisins

1 (4 ounce) jar macadamia nuts

Melt bark or chocolate in microwave or double broiler. Stir in cranberries and nuts. Pour into jellyroll pan lined with foil and spread evenly. Refrigerate 1 hour, then break into pieces.

Yield: 1½ pounds

Fruits, Nuts & Mints

This is Christmas: not the tinsel, not the giving and
receiving, not even the carols, but the humble heart
that receives anew the wondrous gift, the Christ.

FRANK McKibben

Meringue Shells

3 egg whites
1 teaspoon vanilla
½ teaspoon cream of tartar

2 dashes salt
1 cup sugar
Mixed fruit, jam, or nut paste

Beat together egg whites, vanilla, cream of tartar, and salt until it forms soft peaks. Begin adding sugar gradually while beating until it forms stiff peaks. All sugar crystals should be dissolved. Drop by spoonfuls onto parchment paper–lined baking sheet. Using spoon, form a scallop or depression in each meringue. Bake at 275 degrees for about 30 minutes or until very slightly brown. Turn off oven but keep oven door closed and allow meringues to cool and dry for about 2 hours. When ready to serve, spoon mixed fruit, jam, or nut paste into each depression.

Yield: about 2 dozen

Reindeer Tracks

3 cups milk chocolate chips
½ stick butter
1 (14 ounce) can sweetened
    condensed milk

1 teaspoon vanilla
2 cups salted mixed nuts (chopped)
Walnut or pecan halves

In heavy saucepan, melt together chocolate, butter, and milk. Remove from heat when smooth and stir in vanilla and mixed nuts. Drop by spoonfuls onto waxed paper and press a nut half into each.

Yield: 3 dozen

Festive 3-Layer Holiday Mints

1 (14 ounce) can sweetened
  condensed milk
1 stick butter
Dash salt

1 cup milk chocolate candy coating
  disks
1 cup red candy coating disks
1 cup green candy coating disks
½ teaspoon mint extract

Line 8 x 8-inch baking dish with parchment paper. Spray with all-purpose cooking spray and set aside. Melt milk, butter, salt, and milk chocolate disks together. When smooth, pour into baking dish and set into freezer for 30 minutes. Melt red candy disks and pour over first layer. Return to freezer for 30 minutes. Melt green disks along with mint flavoring and pour over first two layers. Chill well. Lift out of pan and invert onto cutting board. Remove parchment and cut into cubes.

Yield: 2 dozen

Christmas Party Mints

1 (8 ounce) package cream cheese
2 pounds powdered sugar

½ teaspoon mint-flavored oil or
    extract

Bring cream cheese to room temperature by leaving out of refrigerator for 2 hours. Stir in sugar and flavoring. Shape into small balls, or press into candy shapes to set.

Yield: about 100

Peach Jellies

4 ripe, pitted, peeled peaches
1 tablespoon lime juice
¼ teaspoon salt

2 cups sugar, divided
3 tablespoons liquid pectin

Combine peaches, lime juice, and salt in blender until very smooth. Pour into heavy medium saucepan and add ½ cup sugar. Bring to very mild bubble, stirring constantly until thickened, about 15 minutes. Add remaining sugar and pectin. Bring mixture to 200 degrees and cook for another 10 minutes, stirring constantly. Pour into plastic wrap–lined, 8 x 11-inch baking dish and refrigerate overnight. The following day, invert candy onto lightly sugared board. Peel plastic off and sprinkle sugar lightly so that both sides are sugared. Cut into squares using a slightly warm knife and store in refrigerator.

Yield: about 2 dozen

Orange Candied Walnuts

¼ cup water
4 tablespoons orange juice
1 tablespoon light corn syrup
1½ cups sugar

Dash salt
¼ cup fresh orange zest
3 cups walnut halves

In heavy saucepan, combine water, juice, corn syrup, sugar, and salt. Bring to soft-ball stage (236 degrees). Remove from heat and stir in orange zest and walnuts, coating well. With a slotted spoon, remove walnuts onto parchment-lined cookie sheet and spread out to set.

Yield: 1 pound

Snowflakes

1 cup flour
1 cup finely chopped walnuts
½ cup light corn syrup

½ cup shortening
⅔ cup brown sugar

Blend flour and nuts. Bring corn syrup, shortening, and sugar to boil over medium heat, stirring constantly. Remove from heat and gradually add flour/nut mixture. Drop batter by teaspoonfuls onto lightly greased cookie sheet. Bake only a few cookies at a time at 375 degrees for 5 to 6 minutes. (They will spread out while baking into a very thin pattern.) Allow to stand for 5 minutes before removing from baking sheet.

Yield: 1½ dozen

Sugar Dandies

½ stick butter
½ cup brown sugar
½ teaspoon nutmeg
1 teaspoon cinnamon

¼ teaspoon salt
2 tablespoons water
3 cups pecan or walnut halves

Melt butter in 9 x 13-inch baking dish in microwave. Stir in sugar, spices, salt, and water. Microwave on high for 1 minute. Stir in nuts until well coated. Microwave for 4 to 5 additional minutes, stirring after each minute. Spread nuts on waxed paper to cool.

Yield: 3 cups

Cinnamon Nuts

3 cups unsalted mixed nuts
½ cup powdered sugar

2 teaspoons cinnamon

Combine nuts, sugar, and cinnamon in plastic bag. Shake to coat nuts well. Spread onto cookie sheet and bake at 285 degrees for 1 hour, stirring occasionally.

Yield: 3 cups

Yule Cups

1 pound high-quality milk chocolate
1 pound high-quality dark chocolate
1 pound high-quality white chocolate

Nuts, dried fruit, or peppermint stick
  slivers

Melt each kind of chocolate separately. When smooth and liquid, pour into mini muffin tins lined with candy wrappers. Fill to half. Place piece of dried fruit, nut, or peppermint stick atop each candy before chocolate hardens.

Yield: 3 pounds

Chocolate-Dipped Dried Apricots

1 (12 ounce) bag white, semisweet, or milk chocolate chips
1 tablespoon vegetable shortening
Dash salt
2 dozen whole dried apricots

Melt chocolate, shortening, and salt in microwave on low burner until smooth. Dip base of each apricot until coated about halfway up. Lay each apricot on waxed paper to harden.

Yield: 2 dozen

Christmas Date Roll

3 cups sugar
1 cup whole milk
1 tablespoon butter
½ teaspoon salt

1½ cups pitted and chopped dates
1 teaspoon vanilla
1 cup chopped pecans
½ cup coconut (optional)

In heavy saucepan, combine first 4 ingredients and bring to soft-ball stage (236 degrees). Add dates and cook gently another 3 minutes. Stir in vanilla and remove from heat. Cool mixture in pan until lukewarm. Beat until creamy while gradually adding nuts. Turn out onto flat surface and form into log roll. Roll log in coconut if desired. Chill and cut into slices when well chilled.

Yield: 2 dozen slices

Candied Citrus Peel

Rind from 6 oranges or 6 grapefruits
  (most of white membrane removed)
2 teaspoons salt
2 cups sugar

½ cup water
Dash salt
Fine granulated sugar for dusting

Divide rind into large sections and submerge in large bowl of salted, cold water for 6 to 8 hours. Drain and rinse rind. Cover rind with cold water in heavy saucepan and bring to a boil. Drain and repeat twice more. (The rind will become less bitter with each repetition.) When cool enough to handle, cut rind into 2-inch strips. In saucepan, combine rind and sugar with ½ cup water and dash of salt. Stir constantly on medium heat until sugar is completely dissolved and rind is translucent. Drain well. Roll in fine granulated sugar, shaking off excess before laying on cooling rack to dry.

Yield: 2 cups

Fruity No-Bakes

3 cups mixed dried fruit
½ cup candied orange or grapefruit
  rind
½ cup candied cherries
1 cup chopped nuts (walnuts or
  pecans)

Dash salt
3 tablespoons orange juice
Powdered sugar for dusting

In food processor, coarsely grind all ingredients but juice. Then add enough juice to allow mixture to stick together. Press into greased 8-inch square pan and chill overnight. Dust lightly with powdered sugar and cut into cubes.

Yield: 2 dozen

Almond Dainties

2 cups whole almonds
½ cup sugar
¼ cup butter

½ teaspoon salt
1 teaspoon vanilla

In heavy saucepan, combine all ingredients and cook over medium heat for about 15 minutes, stirring constantly. Mixture should turn a golden hue when done. Spread mixture onto greased flat surface to cool.

Yield: 2 cups

Lemon Dainties

3 egg whites
1 teaspoon vanilla
½ teaspoon cream of tartar

2 dashes salt
1 teaspoon lemon extract
1 cup sugar

Beat together egg whites, vanilla, cream of tartar, salt, and lemon flavoring until mixture forms soft peaks. Begin adding sugar gradually while beating until stiff peaks are formed. (All sugar crystals should be dissolved.) Drop by spoonfuls onto parchment paper–lined baking sheet. Bake at 275 degrees for about 30 minutes or until very slightly brown. Turn off oven but keep door closed to allow meringues to cool and dry for about 2 hours.

Yield: about 2 dozen

Raspberry Jingle Bells

2 sticks butter
1½ cups sugar
2 egg yolks
2½ cups flour

8 ounces raspberry jam
1½ cups chopped macadamia nuts
Powdered sugar for dusting

Cream together butter, sugar, and egg yolks. Work flour in gently (you may need to use your hands). When smooth dough is formed, press into ungreased jelly roll pan. Bake at 350 degrees until very lightly brown, about 15 minutes. Spread jam over dough while it is still hot. Allow to cool for about 10 minutes, then sprinkle with nuts. Dust with powdered sugar and let mixture set up. Cut into small squares.

Yield: 3 dozen

Raisin Cups

1 roll sugar cookie dough
1 cup raisins
¼ cup water
½ cup sugar

1 tablespoon butter
2 tablespoons light corn syrup
¼ teaspoon salt

Gently press dough into mini muffin cups and make a depression in the center. Bake at temperature directed on package until golden brown. Remove and set aside to cool. In small saucepan, combine remaining ingredients. Bring to soft boil for 5 minutes. Remove from heat and cool by stirring. As mixture begins to thicken, spoon small amount into each cookie cup. Allow to cool before removing from muffin tin.

Yield: 2 dozen

Easy Chocolate-Covered Cherries

1 (16 ounce) jar maraschino cherries
   in syrup (well-drained)
2 cups chocolate chips
Dash salt

1 tablespoon butter
¼ cup white chocolate chips
½ teaspoon vegetable shortening

With paper towel, pat drained cherries until dry. Melt chocolate, salt, and butter together until smooth and creamy. Pour in cherries and stir to coat. With slotted spoon lift cherries out individually, shaking off excess. Place on metal strainer to cool and set. When hardened, melt white chocolate chips and shortening. Using a spoon, drizzle white chocolate in streaks across milk chocolate–covered cherries.

Yield: 1 pound

Stuffed Dates

2 cups large pitted dates
½ cup finely chopped walnuts

1 cup powdered sugar

Open each date lengthwise and liberally sprinkle with nuts. Press date closed around nuts and roll in powdered sugar to coat.

Yield: 1 dozen

Divinity Candy

3 cups sugar
1 cup light corn syrup
½ cup hot water
½ teaspoon salt

3 egg whites
1 cup finely chopped nuts
1 teaspoon vanilla

In heavy saucepan, cook sugar, corn syrup, water, and salt to hard-ball stage (265 degrees). Beat egg whites until stiff and slowly pour syrup over them. Beat until creamy then add nuts and vanilla. Drop by spoonfuls onto waxed paper to set up.

Yield: 3 dozen

Peppermint Meringues

3 egg whites
1 teaspoon vanilla
½ teaspoon cream of tartar
2 dashes salt

3 to 4 drops peppermint extract
Red food coloring
1 cup sugar

Beat together egg whites, vanilla, cream of tartar, salt, and flavoring until the mixture forms soft peaks. Begin adding sugar gradually and continue beating until the mixture forms stiff peaks. (All sugar crystals should be dissolved.) Drop by spoonfuls onto parchment paper–lined baking sheet. Bake at 275 degrees for about 30 minutes or until very slightly brown. Turn off oven but keep door closed to allow meringues to cool and dry for about 2 hours.

Yield: about 2 dozen

Fresh Raspberry Bark

1 pint firm, fresh raspberries (well-chilled)

1 pound high-quality white chocolate

1 tablespoon vegetable shortening

Dash salt

Spread raspberries evenly in parchment-lined jelly roll pan. Slowly melt white chocolate, shortening, and salt in heavy saucepan. When smooth, allow to cool slightly. Pour evenly over fruit and allow to set in refrigerator. Enjoy within 2 days, as raspberries spoil quickly!

Yield: 1 pound

Candy Confections

May you have the gladness
of Christmas, which is Hope.

Ava V. Hendricks

Sweet 'N' Salty Chocolate Drops

1 cup butterscotch chips
1 cup milk chocolate chips
1 tablespoon vegetable shortening

1 cup dry-roasted salted peanuts
1 cup broken up salted pretzel sticks

Melt chips in saucepan with shortening. Stir in peanuts and pretzels and drop by mounds on waxed paper and allow to harden.

Yield: 2 dozen

Meringue Christmas Trees

2 egg whites, room temperature
¼ teaspoon salt
¼ teaspoon cream of tartar
1 cup powdered sugar

1 teaspoon vanilla
Green food coloring
1 cup melted dipping chocolate
½ cup chopped nuts

Beat egg whites at high speed until very frothy. Add salt and cream of tartar. Begin adding powdered sugar a tablespoon at a time. When sugar is incorporated, add in vanilla and green food coloring. Beat until very stiff, about 10 minutes. Fill pastry bag or large re-sealable food storage bag with whites. Working on parchment-covered cookie sheet, pipe whites into spirals, about 2 inches at base and ending in a peak, about 3 inches tall. (They will look like little Christmas trees.) Bake at 250 degrees for one hour, then turn off oven and allow trees to cool slowly. When completely cool and hard, melt chocolate and dip only the base of each tree first in chocolate, then in nuts. Set back on parchment to set.

Yield: 2 dozen

Holiday Crunch

4 cups broken pretzels (large chucks)
4 cups white chocolate chips

1 (14 ounce) can sweetened
    condensed milk
1½ cups dried fruit (diced)

Break up pretzels into large bowl. In heavy saucepan, mix chocolate and condensed milk. Heat slowly, stirring constantly, until mixture is smooth and melted. Quickly stir into pretzels until all are coated. Spread out into thin layer on parchment-lined cookie sheet. Sprinkle with dried fruit and press fruit into the chocolate. Chill and break up into pieces.

Yield: 1½ pounds

Italian Cinnamon Pops

½ pound semisweet dipping chocolate
Dash salt
1 teaspoon instant coffee crystals

12 cinnamon-flavored lollipops
1 cup white chocolate chips
¼ cup cinnamon red hot candies

Melt chocolate together with salt and coffee crystals. Dip each lollipop to cover candy. Place on mesh to drip dry, decorating with red hot candies before chocolate hardens. Melt white chocolate and streak across chocolate pops for contrast.

Yield: 12

Christmas Corn Crunch

3 quarts popped corn
3 cups corn cereal squares
3 cups broken up corn chips

1 (10 ounce) bag peanut butter or
  butterscotch chips
1 (10 ounce) bag milk or dark
  chocolate chips
2 tablespoons vegetable shortening

In large bowl, combine popcorn, cereal, and corn chips. In saucepan over medium heat, melt chips and vegetable shortening together. Stir until smooth. Pour over popcorn mixture and toss to coat. Spread onto 2 greased baking sheets. Cool and break into pieces.

Yield: 9 cups

Chocolate-Dipped Candy Canes

½ pound bittersweet dipping
   chocolate

12 large candy canes or peppermint
   sticks

Melt chocolate in deep bowl or saucepan. Holding candy cane by its stem, dip crook into the chocolate. Place flat on mesh to drain and set.

Yield: 12

Peanut Butter Santas

2 sticks butter or 1 cup margarine
1 (12 ounce) jar peanut butter
1½ cups graham cracker crumbs

1 teaspoon vanilla
1 pound powdered sugar
1 pound dipping chocolate

Combine first 5 ingredients until well blended. Press into Santa candy molds. Once set, pop out of molds and dip in melted chocolate. Shake off excess and place on waxed paper to harden.

Yield: 10 large or 20 small Santas

Christmas Eve Caramel Corn

2 cups packed light brown sugar
½ cup light corn syrup
2 sticks butter or 1 cup margarine
¼ teaspoon cream of tartar

1 teaspoon salt
1 teaspoon baking soda
6 quarts freshly popped corn

Combine first 5 ingredients in heavy 2-quart saucepan. Stir over medium heat until boiling. Cook for about 5 minutes to hard-ball stage (265 degrees). Remove from heat and stir in baking soda. Pour over popped corn in large shallow roasting pan, stirring until all the corn is well coated. Bake at 200 degrees for 1 hour, stirring 2 or 3 times during baking. Turn at once onto waxed paper to cool.

Yield: 6 quarts

Christmas Kettle Corn

2 cups sugar
1 cup water
2 tablespoons butter

Dash salt
Food coloring, if desired
5 quarts popped corn

Combine sugar, water, butter, and salt in heavy sauce pan. Cook to hard-ball stage (265 degrees) or until spoonful of mixture forms a hard ball in cold water. Add red or green food coloring if desired. Pour mixture over popped corn and stir to coat.

Yield: 5 quarts

Reindeer Mix

1 cup miniature salted pretzels
1 cup corn squares cereal
1 cup rice squares cereal
1 cup salted mixed nuts

1 cup Boston Baked Beans candy
1 cup chocolate-coated candies
1 cup dried cranberries

Mix all ingredients together thoroughly and store in airtight container.

Yield: 7 cups

Popcorn Balls

2 cups sugar
1½ cups water
½ teaspoon salt
½ cup corn syrup

1 teaspoon vinegar
1 teaspoon vanilla
5 quarts popped corn

In large, heavy saucepan, combine sugar, water, salt, corn syrup, and vinegar. Cook to hard-ball stage (265 degrees). Stir in vanilla. Slowly pour hot mixture over popped corn and stir to coat corn. Butter hands generously and shape corn into balls.

Yield: 15 to 20 balls

Chocolate Popcorn Balls

1½ cups sugar
½ cup corn syrup
⅔ cup water
½ cup molasses
½ stick butter

½ teaspoon salt
3 ounces melted chocolate
1 teaspoon vanilla
5 quarts popped corn

Combine sugar, corn syrup, and water in heavy saucepan. Cook to hard-ball stage (270 degrees). Add in molasses, butter, and salt. Continue cooking to hard-crack (brittle) stage (280 degrees). Add in melted chocolate and vanilla. Pour over freshly popped corn and mix well. Form into balls.

Yield: 15 to 20 balls

Cracker Corn Jumble

1 cup molasses
1 cup sugar
1 teaspoon vinegar
2 tablespoons water
1 tablespoon butter

½ teaspoon salt
½ teaspoon baking soda
5 quarts popped corn
1 cup peanuts

In heavy saucepan, combine molasses, sugar, vinegar, water, butter, and salt.
Cook, stirring constantly, to hard-ball stage (265 degrees), or until spoonful of
mixture forms hard ball in cold water. Remove from heat and add baking soda.
Mixture will foam. Pour over mixed popcorn and nuts and allow to cool before
breaking into chunks.

Yield: 5 quarts

Cinnamon Candy Apples

6 wooden skewers
6 crisp tart apples (Granny Smith
    work well)
1½ cups sugar

2 cups light corn syrup
Light dash salt
Red food coloring
8 to 10 drops cinnamon extract

Insert skewer into base end of each apple. Combine sugar, corn syrup, salt, food coloring, and cinnamon extract in heavy saucepan and cook at gentle boil to hard-crack stage (300 degrees), or when brittle ribbons form when spooned into cold water. Remove from heat and swirl each apple in syrup until well coated. Gently shake off excess and place each apple on greased surface to set.

Yield: 6 apples

Caramel Apples

6 medium tart apples (use Granny
    Smith or Honey Crisp)
6 popsicle sticks or apple skewers

2 (11 ounce) bags wrapped caramels
2 cups coarsely chopped walnuts

Insert skewer into the base of each apple. Unwrap caramels and melt according
to package instructions. Dip each apple in caramel to coat. Then sprinkle with
chopped nuts. Set on waxed paper to cool and set.

Yield: 6 apples

Chocolate-Dipped Candy Canes

1 (12 ounce) bag semisweet or milk
   chocolate chips
1 tablespoon vegetable shortening

Dash salt
20 large candy canes

Melt chocolate chips and shortening in microwave or slowly over burner. Add salt. Dip the crook and halfway down stem of each cane into the chocolate. Shake off excess and lay on waxed paper to harden.

Yield: 20

Chocolate-Dipped Pretzels

1 (12 ounce) bag white, semisweet, or milk chocolate chips
1 tablespoon vegetable shortening

2 dozen large stick or twisted thick pretzels

Melt chocolate and shortening in microwave, or on low burner, until smooth. Dip base of each pretzel until coated about halfway up. Lay on waxed paper to harden.

Yield: 2 dozen

Chocolate Spoons

1 (12 ounce) bag milk chocolate chips   ½ cup large grain sugar
1 tablespoon vegetable shortening   ½ cup crushed candy canes
12 to 15 clear plastic spoons

Melt chocolate chips and shortening together and dip end of each spoon in chocolate mixture until coated. Let set. Repeat with second coat of chocolate. Sprinkle with sugar and candy cane bits. Place on waxed paper to set.

Yield: 1 dozen

Chocolate-Covered Sugar Cubes

1 cup milk chocolate chips
1 teaspoon vegetable shortening

1 (16 ounce) box sugar cubes

Melt chocolate and shortening together. Using small tongs, dip sugar cubes in warm chocolate. Shake off excess and let drain and set over mesh strainer to keep chocolate from pooling. Drop one or two into a cup of coffee and enjoy!

Yield: 20 cubes

Holiday Wreath Candy

1 stick butter
Dash salt
3 cups miniature marshmallows
1 teaspoon vanilla

Green food coloring
3 cups cornflakes cereal
½ cup red hot cinnamon candies

In large, heavy saucepan, stir together butter, salt, and marshmallows. Add vanilla and food coloring. Then stir in cornflakes. Drop by spoonfuls onto waxed paper and form into little wreaths. While still warm and sticky, decorate with cinnamon candies.

Yield: 2 dozen

Notes

Notes

Notes

Notes

Notes

Notes

Notes

Index

O taste and see that
the LORD is good.
PSALM 34:8 KJV